9-1 GCSE REVISION NOTES

9-1 GCSE NOTES ROBERT LOUIS STEVENSON'S *DR JEKYLL & MR HYDE* - Study guide (All chapters, page-by-page analysis)

by Joe Broadfoot

All rights reserved

Copyright © Joe Broadfoot, 2016

The right of Joe Broadfoot to be identified as the author of this work has been asserted in accordance with Section 77 of the Copyright, Designs and Patents Act 1988

ISBN-13: 978-1537412528

9-1 GCSE REVISION NOTES – JEKYLL & HYDE

ISBN-10:
1537412523

CONTENTS
INTRODUCTION/CRITERIA 3
ESSAY PLANNING 4
NEW SPECIFICATION 6
CHAPTER ONE 12
SAMPLE QUESTION 15
EXEMPLAR ANNOTATION/STUDENT ACTIVITIES 16
CHAPTER TWO 17
CHAPTER THREE 19
CHAPTER FOUR 20
CHAPTER FIVE 22
CHAPTER SIX 24
CHAPTER SEVEN 26
CHAPTER EIGHT 27
CHAPTER NINE 29
CHAPTER TEN 31
ESSAY TIPS 34
GLOSSARY 39

Brief Introduction

This book is aimed at GCSE students of English Literature who are studying Robert Louis Stevenson's *The Strange Case of Dr Jekyll and Mr Hyde*. The focus is on what examiners are looking for, especially since the changes to the curriculum in 2015, and here you will find each chapter covered in detail. I hope this will help you and be a valuable tool in your studies and revision.

Criteria for high marks

Make sure you use appropriate critical language (see glossary of literary terms at the back). You need your argument to be fluent, well-structured and coherent. Stay focused!

Analyse and explore the use of form, structure and the language. Explore how these aspects affect the meaning.

Make connections between texts and look at different interpretations. Explore their strengths and weaknesses. Don't forget to use supporting references to strengthen your argument.

Analyse and explore the context.

9-1 GCSE REVISION NOTES – JEKYLL & HYDE

Best essay practice
There are so many way to write an essay. Many schools use **PEE** for paragraphs: point/evidence/explain. Others use **PETER**: point/evidence/technique/explain/reader; **PEEL**: point, example, explain, link; **PEEE**: point/evidence/explain/explore. Whichever method you use, make sure you mention the **writer's effects**. This generally is what most students forget to add. You must think of what the writer is trying to achieve by using a particular technique and what is actually achieved. Do not just spot techniques and note them. You may get some credit for using appropriate technology, but unless you can comment on the effect created on the reader and/or the writer's intention, you will miss out on most of the marks available.

Essay planning
In order to write a good essay it is necessary to plan. In fact, it is best to quite formulaic in an exam situation, as you won't have much time to get started. Therefore I will ask you to learn the following acronym: **DATMC (Definition, Application, Terminology, Main, Conclusion**. Some schools call it: **GSLMC (General, Specific, Link, Main, Conclusion)**, but it amounts to the same thing. The first three letters concern the introduction. (Of course, the alternative is to leave some blank lines and write your introduction after you have completed the main body of your essay, but it is probably not advisable for most students).
Let us first look at the following exam question, which is on poetry (of course, the same essay-planning principles apply to essays on novels and plays as well).
QUESTION: Explore how the poet conveys **feelings** in the poem.

STEP ONE: Identify the **keyword** in the question. (I have already done this, by highlighting it in **bold**). If you are following GSLMC, you now need to make a **general statement** about what feelings are. Alternatively, if you're following DATMC, simply **define** 'feelings'. For example, 'Feelings are emotion states or reactions or vague, irrationals ideas and beliefs'.

STEP TWO: If you are following GSLMC, you now need to make a **specific statement** linking feelings (or whatever else you've defined) to how they appear in the poem. Alternatively, if you're following DATMC, simply define which 'feelings' **apply** in this poem. For example, 'The feelings love, fear and guilt appear in this poem, and are expressed by the speaker in varying degrees.'

STEP THREE: If you are following GSLMC, you now need to make a **link statement** identifying the methods used to convey the feelings (or whatever else you've defined) in the poem. Alternatively, if you're following DATMC, simply define which **techniques** are used to convey 'feelings' in this poem. For example, 'The poet primarily uses alliteration to emphasise his heightened emotional state, while hyperbole and enjambment also help to convey the sense that the speaker is descending into a state of madness.

STEP FOUR: Whether you are following GSLMC or DATMC, the next stage is more or less the same. The main part of the essay involves writing around **six paragraphs**, using whichever variation of PEEE you prefer. In my example, I will use **Point, Evidence, Exploration, Effect** on the listener. To make your essay even stronger, try to use your quotations chronologically. It will be easier for the examiner to follow, which means you are more likely to achieve a higher grade. To be more specific, I recommend that you take and analyse two quotations from the beginning of the poem, two from the middle, and two at the end.

9-1 GCSE REVISION NOTES – JEKYLL & HYDE

STEP FIVE: Using Carol Ann Duffy's poem, 'Stealing', here's an example of how you could word one of your six paragraphs:
(POINT) 'Near the beginning of the poem, the speaker's determination is expressed.' **(EVIDENCE)** 'This is achieved through the words: 'Better off dead than giving in'.
(EXPLORATION). The use of 'dead' emphasizes how far the speaker is prepared to go in pursuit of what he wants, although there is a sense that he is exaggerating (hyperbole). **(EFFECT)** The listener senses that the speaker may be immature given how prone he is to exaggerate his own bravery.

STEP SIX: After writing five or more paragraphs like the one above, it will be time to write a **conclusion**. In order to do that, it is necessary to sum up your previous points and evaluate them. This is not the time to introduce additional quotations. Here is an example of what I mean: 'To conclude, the poet clearly conveys the speaker's anger. Although the listener will be reluctant to completely sympathise with a thief, there is a sense that the speaker is suffering mentally, which makes him an interesting and partially a sympathetic character. By using a dramatic monologue form, the poet effectively conveys the speaker's mental anguish, which makes it easier to more deeply understand what first appears to be inexplicable acts of violence.

Other tips

Make your studies active!

Don't just sit there reading! Never forget to annotate, annotate and annotate!

All page references refer to the 2000 reprinted paperback edition of *Dr Jekyll and Mr Hyde* published by Wandsworth Classics, London (ISBN: 978-1-85326-061-2).

The Strange Case of Dr Jekyll and Mr Hyde AQA (New specification starting in 2015)

If you're studying for an AQA qualification in English Literature, there's a good chance your teachers will choose this text to study. There are good reasons for that: it's moralistic in that the text encourages us to think about right and wrong.

Dr Jekyll and Mr Hyde is one of the texts listed on Paper 1. More about that particular paper later.

The other paper, Paper 2, needs to be completed in 2 hours 15 minutes. Your writing on the essay will only be part of the exam, however, and for the rest of time you will need to write about poetry: two poems categorised as 'Unseen Poetry' and two poems from the AQA anthology.

AQA have given students a choice of 12 set texts for the Modern Texts section of the exam paper. There are 6 plays: JB Priestley's *An Inspector Calls*, Willy Russell's *Blood Brothers*, Alan Bennett's *The History Boys*, Dennis Kelly's *DNA*, Simon Stephens's script of *The Curious Incident of the Dog* in the *Night-Time*, and Shelagh Delaney's *A Taste of Honey*. Alternatively, students can chose to write on the following 6 novels: William Golding's *Lord of the Flies*, AQA's Anthology

9-1 GCSE REVISION NOTES – JEKYLL & HYDE

called *Telling Tales*, George Orwell's *Animal Farm*, Kazuo Ishiguro's *Never Let Me Go*, Meera Syal's *Anita and Me*, and Stephen Kelman's *Pigeon English*. Answering one essay question on one of the above is worth a total of 34 marks, which includes 4 for vocabulary, spelling, punctuation and grammar. In other words, this section is worth 21.25% of your total grade at GCSE.

AQA have produced a poetry anthology entitled *Poems, Past and Present*, which includes 30 poems. Rather than study all 30, students are to study one of the two clusters of 15, which concentrate on common themes. There are two themes which students can choose from: Love and relationships, or power and conflict. Within the chosen thematic cluster, students must study all 15 poems and be prepared to write on any of them. Answering this section is worth 18.75% of your total GCSE grade.

The 'unseen poetry' section is more demanding, in that students will not know what to expect. However, as long as they are prepared to comment and compare different poems in terms of their content, theme, structure and language, students should be ready for whatever the exam can throw at them. This section is worth 20% of your total grade at GCSE.

Paper 2 itself makes up 60% of your total grade or, in other words, 96 raw marks. Just under half of those marks, 44 to be exact (27.5% of 60%), can be gained from analysing how the writer uses language, form and structure to create effects. To get a high grade, it is necessary for students to use appropriate literary terms, like metaphors, similes and so on.

AO1 accounts for 36 marks of the total of 96 (22.5% of the 60% for Paper 2, to be exact). To score highly on AO1, students need to provide an informed personal response, using quotations to support their point of view.

AO3 is all about context and, like Paper 1, only 7.5% of the total mark is awarded for this knowledge (12 marks). Similarly, AO4 (which is about spelling, punctuation and grammar) only accounts for 2.5% of the total (4 marks).

Let's return to Paper One now, as it's the main focus of this book. One of the difficulties with Paper 1 is the language. That can't be helped, bearing in mind that part A of the exam paper involves answering questions on Shakespeare, whereas part B is all about the 19th-century novel.

To further complicate things, the education system is in a state of flux: that means we have to be ready for constant change. Of course, everyone had got used to grades A,B and C meaning a pass. It was simple, it was straightforward and nearly everyone understood it. Please be prepared that from this day henceforward, the top grade will now be known as 9. A grade 4 will be a pass, and anything below that will be found and anything above it will be a pass. Hopefully, that's not too confusing for anyone!

Now onto the exam itself. As I said, Paper 1 consists of Shakespeare and the 19th-century novel. Like Paper 2, it is a written closed-book exam (in other words you are not allowed to have the texts with you), which lasts one hour 45

9-1 GCSE REVISION NOTES – JEKYLL & HYDE

minutes. You can score 64 marks, which amounts to 40% of your GCSE grade.

In section B, students will be expected to write in detail about an extract from the novel they have studied in class and then write about the novel as a whole. Just for the record, the choices of novel are the following: *The Strange Case of Dr Jekyll and Mr Hyde* by Robert Louis Stevenson, *A Christmas Carol* and *Great Expectations* by Charles Dickens, *Jane Eyre* by Charlotte Brontë, *Frankenstein* by Mary Shelley, *Pride and Prejudice* by Jane Austin, and *The Sign of Four* by Sir Arthur Conan Doyle.

Another important thing to consider is the fact that for section B of Paper 1, you will not be assessed on Assessment Objective 4 (AO4), which involves spelling, punctuation, grammar and vocabulary. This will be assessed on section A of Paper 1, which is about Shakespeare, and it will be worth 2.5% of your overall GCSE grade. In terms of raw marks, it is worth 4 out of 64. So for once, we need not concern ourselves with what is affectionately known as 'SPAG' too much on this part of Paper 1.

However, it is necessary to use the correct literary terminology wherever possible to make sure we maximise our marks on Assessment Objective2 (AO2). AO2 tests how well we can analyse language form and structure. Additionally, we are expected to state the effect the writer tried to create and how it impacts on the reader.

This brings me onto Assessment Objective 1 (AO1), which involves you writing a personal response to the text. It is important that you use quotations to backup your points of view. Like AO2, AO1 is worth 15% of your GCSE on Paper 1.

Assessment Objective 3 (AO3) is worth half of that, but nevertheless it is important to comment on context to make sure you get as much of the 7.5% up for grabs as you can.

So just to make myself clear, there are 30 marks available in section B for your answer on the 19th-century novel. Breaking it down even further, you will get 12 marks maximum the backing up your personal opinion with quotations, an additional 12 marks for analysing the writer's choice of words for effect (not forgetting to use appropriate terminology - more on that see the glossary at the back of this book), and six marks for discussing context.

As you can see, we've got a lot to get through so without further ado let's get on with the actual text itself and possible exam questions.

Previous exam questions

Notwithstanding the governmental changes to the grading system, it is still good practice to go over previous exam papers. To make sure that you meet AQA's learning objectives and get a high mark, make sure you go into the exam knowing something about the following:

- the plot

9-1 GCSE REVISION NOTES – JEKYLL & HYDE

- the characters
- the theme
- selected quotations/details
- exam skills

<u>Page-by-page analysis</u>

Chapter One

The opening chapter is entitled: 'The Story of the Door', so we should consider any symbolism conveyed by it. Our first thoughts may lead us to think of two spheres of life: the domestic and the world outside. The door is the portal that allows a person to take on a different guise once they pass through it, especially in this novella. This ties in with the idea of the 'Gothic double', which suggests that doppelgängers exist. Not only that, the idea is threatening, so adds suspense to the narrative.

The first character we encounter is Mr Utterson. We are told he is 'a man of rugged counternance, that was never lighted by a smile' (3). In short, he does not appear to be the sort of person who would be much fun to be with. However, although he lacks the light of a smile, 'something eminently human beaconed from his eye' when 'the wine was to his taste' (3). This shows that he is tolerant of others and warms to them under the influence of alcohol. It is almost as if he needs a drug like that to release his inner self.

We then hear about his relationship with 'Mr Richard Enfield, his distant kinsman' or relative (3). They have 'Sunday walks' together although they couldn't be more different from each other (3). There is a suggestion of something almost religious about their relationship, given that their meetings take place on a Sunday.

The pair's walk takes them to 'a busy quarter of London' and a street that 'shone out in contrast to its dingy neighborhood, like a fire in a forest (4). The recurring light imagery reminds us that although fire is attractive and warm, it is also dangerous if it gets out of control. The theme of self-control, or a lack of it is very much present in the novella. We've already discovered that Enfield is 'a well-known man about town', unlike Utterson, who is completely opposite.

Using the technique of the embedded narrative, Enfield begins to relate the strange happenings that have occurred at this very scene. The embedded narrative adds realism to the story, making it appear more credible, like a witness account of a crime.

In fact, it is a crime that Enfield has witnessed, as he tells Utterson of a man trampling 'calmly over a girl's body' (4). Enfield compares the man to 'some damned Juggernaut', which alludes to an old practice of driving an image of the god Krishna through the streets of India on a cart for devoted followers to throw themselves in front of it (5). These devotees would be crushed. Through this imagery, we get an idea of the violence and almost religious fervor of the man behind the horse and cart.

Enfield detains the man who 'made no resistance' but gives him such an 'ugly' look that it makes him break into a cold sweat (5). A doctor 'with a strong Edinburgh accent' appears, who is probably good at his job if he were trained in the Scottish capital's famous nineteenth-century medical school

9-1 GCSE REVISION NOTES – JEKYLL & HYDE

(5). However, Enfield disparagingly refers to him as 'the Sawbones', referring to the crude medical practice of amputating limbs (5). This seems to suggest that Enfield has little confidence in doctors' opinions. Although he describes the doctor as 'emotional as a bagpipe', he also notes that 'the desire to kill' the man who ran over the little girl' (5). This is matched by the women who surround the mad driver of the cart, who are 'as wild as harpies' (5). This reference to Greek mythological beasts shows how transformed they are by what's happened. Transformation is a key theme in the novella.

Nevertheless, the mad driver remains unperturbed by it all, 'carrying it off [...] like Satan' (5). He clearly is a diabolical character in every sense of the word. Additionally, he rather callously asks them to 'name' their ' 'figure' of compensation (5). However, Enfield is shocked by the 'name' he 'can't mention' on the cheque (5). The unspeakable is often used in gothic literature to add suspense and dread to the narrative.

Enfield adds that the unmentionable man 'is the very pink of the proprieties' (6). Using the alliterative 'p', the narrative emphasises how perfect this person is; he is not someone who would normally be associated with a mad driver. No wonder, Enfield suspects 'blackmail' (6). He thinks this poor man is experiencing considerable difficulties, putting him in 'Queer Street' (6).

To conclude the chapter, Enfield reveals that the mad driver's name is 'Hyde' (7). He describes him as 'an extraordinary-looking man'. Enfield and Utterson agree never to mention this incident again.

SAMPLE QUESTION: Now read the following extract (in bold), before answering the following question: how does Stevenson present Utterson as a man to be trusted (in the extract and in the novel as a whole)?

Mr. Utterson the lawyer was a man of a rugged countenance that was never lighted by a smile; cold, scanty and embarrassed in discourse; backward in sentiment; lean, long, dusty, dreary and yet somehow lovable. At friendly meetings, and when the wine was to his taste, something eminently human beaconed from his eye; something indeed which never found its way into his talk, but which spoke not only in these silent symbols of the after-dinner face, but more often and loudly in the acts of his life. He was austere with himself; drank gin when he was alone, to mortify a taste for vintages; and though he enjoyed the theater, had not crossed the doors of one for twenty years. But he had an approved tolerance for others; sometimes wondering, almost with envy, at the high pressure of spirits involved in their misdeeds; and in any extremity inclined to help rather than to reprove. "I incline to Cain's heresy," he used to say quaintly: "I let my brother go to the devil in his own way." In this character, it was frequently his fortune to be the last reputable acquaintance and the last good influence in the lives of downgoing men. And to such as these, so long as they came about his chambers, he never marked a shade of change in his demeanour.

9-1 GCSE REVISION NOTES – JEKYLL & HYDE

EXEMPLAR ANNOTATION

Mr. Utterson the lawyer was a man of a **rugged countenance** that was **never lighted by a smile**; cold, **scanty and embarrassed in discourse**; **backward in sentiment**; **lean, long, dusty, dreary and yet somehow lovable**. At friendly meetings, and **when the wine was to his taste, something eminently human beaconed from his eye**; something indeed which **never found its way into his talk**, but which spoke not only in these silent symbols of the after-dinner face, but more often and loudly in the **acts** of his life. He was austere with himself; drank gin when he was alone, to mortify a taste for vintages; and **though he enjoyed the theater, had not crossed the doors of one for twenty years**. But he had an approved tolerance for others; sometimes **wondering, almost with envy, at the high pressure of spirits involved in their misdeeds**; and in any extremity inclined to help rather than to reprove. "I incline to **Cain's heresy**," he used to say quaintly: "I let my brother go to the devil in his own way." In this character, it was frequently his fortune to be the last reputable acquaintance and the **last good influence in the lives of downgoing men**. And to such as these, so long as they came about his chambers, **he never marked a shade of change in his demeanour**.

Comment [M]: Suggests that he is a tough character, who is weather-worn, which implies he's seen a lot in life.

Comment [M]: Always serious, so a reliable witness to the wildness of the events that follow.

Comment [M]: Not one for idle chatter.

Comment [M]: Not overly sentimental or given to exaggeration

Comment [M]: Despite his appearance and general cold demeanour, it seems he is a loving person deep down.

Comment [M]: He needs alcohol to release his warmer inner self.

Comment [M]: Even when drunk, he remains circumspect verbally. He does, however, express himself his warmer side through his actions.

Comment [M]: Lives a life of self-imposed abstinence.

Comment [M]: He is almost envious of those who enjoy a greater freedom than he does.

Comment [M]: This Biblical reference to Cain, who murdered his brother, suggests that Utterson feels some guilt that he has not done more aid his fellow man. It may also suggest he is envious of others, as Cain killed Abel for that reason.

Comment [M]: Suggests incredibly loyalty and foreshadows the idea that he will be attached to a character facing a

Comment [M]: He has a poker face, so if he judges others it is not noticeable.

ACTIVITY 1: NOW WRITE ABOUT UTTERSON USING THE EXTRACT AND THE NOVEL AS A WHOLE.

ACTIVITY 2: FIND YOUR OWN 300-WORD EXTRACTS FROM THE OTHER CHAPTERS. WRITE YOUR OWN QUESTION AND THEN ANNOTATE THE EXTRACT.

Chapter Two

The chapter is entitled: 'Search for Mr Hyde' and it begins with Mr Utterson sitting 'down to dinner without relish' (7). He is upset about Jekyll's handwritten will, as the 'benefactor' is Edward Hyde (8). Now that he thinks he knows the 'detestable' Hyde, Utterson feels a lot of 'indignation' (8). He thinks it is wrong that Jekyll is leaving his money, should he die first, to a fiend.

With this on his mind, Utterson goes out to consult 'his friend, the great Dr Lanyon' (8). This friend appears to be accustomed to surprises, as his 'shock of hair' has gone 'prematurely white' (8). The colour of his hair could also symbolise a pure moral nature.

Lanyon tells Utterson that Henry Jekyll is full of 'unscientific balderdash' (9). This shows that the pair are poles apart when it comes to science. Their disagreement is so extreme, it would have parted the mythical friends, 'Damon and Pythias', according to Lanyon.

After discovering that Lanyon has no knowledge of Hyde, Utterson decides to be 'Mr Seek' and pursue the man (10). Although Hyde is 'small and very plainly dressed', when tapped on the shoulder, he shrinks 'back with a hissing intake of the breath' (11). This sound imagery makes Hyde appear to be as dangerous as a snake. Hyde may be 'pale and dwarfish', but his snarl that turns 'into a savage laugh' makes him seem a formidable foe (11).

The narrator describes Hyde as giving off 'the impression of deformity without a unnamable malformation' (12). This is a reference to physiognomy, a pseudo-science that maintained

9-1 GCSE REVISION NOTES – JEKYLL & HYDE

that physical appearance played a major part in determining personality. Clearly, the narrative is looking for, but not finding, flaws in Hyde's appearance which would explain his behaviour.

Utterson is 'perplexed' by what he's seen in Hyde and talks to himself (12). He remembers 'the old story of Dr Fell', which refers to a reportedly evil seventeenth-century bishop (12). The name 'Fell' may refer to the Biblical story of man's fall from God's grace, which saw Adam and Eve eat from the Tree of Knowledge. Likewise, Jekyll is intent on experimenting to find out knowledge, judging by his disagreement with a more conventional scientist, Lanyon.

As Utterson returns home, he thinks of how 'wild' Jekyll was 'when he was young' (13). He believes Jekyll must be being blackmailed for 'some old sin' (13). By comparison, Utterson feels his 'past' is 'fairly blameless' (13). However, he feels that Hyde's past must be far worse than Jekyll's and feels a lot of sympathy for his friend. Utterson is determined to do something about the will, as he is afraid that Hyde 'may grow impatient to inherit' Jekyll's fortune (13). This adds suspense, as Jekyll may be in grave danger.

Chapter Three

This chapter is entitled: 'Dr Jekyll was quite at Ease', so the reader will expect to discover more about this character (13).

However, the third person narrative gives us more idea about Utterson's feelings than it does Jekyll's. This adds tension, as Utterson, like the reader, is trying to figure out why the doctor has named Hyde as his will's beneficiary.

Jekyll is described as 'a large, well-made, smooth-faced man of fifty, with something of a slyish glance perhaps' (14). This description makes the reader think that Jekyll is hiding something of his true nature, behind that 'slyish glance' (14).

Utterson continues to probe into what Jekyll regards as 'a private matter' (15). Eventually, Jekyll asks the former to 'promise' to help Hyde, in the event that the doctor is 'no longer here' (15). Utterson agrees to do that. The reader is left on another cliff hanger, as Jekyll's demise appears to be imminent.

9-1 GCSE REVISION NOTES – JEKYLL & HYDE

Chapter Four

We discover that there has been 'a crime of singular ferocity' and the reader can guess that this alludes to the name in chapter's title: 'The Carew Murder Case' (15).

We hear the account of 'a maid-servant', albeit in indirect speech (15). This device makes her version of events mediated. It also adds a little more objectivity to her story.

She describes a street meeting, which she could see from her in window, between 'an aged and beautiful gentleman with white hair' and a 'very small gentleman (15).

The latter, she recognises as Hyde, 'who had once visited her master' (16). Hyde clubs the older man to death 'with ape-like fury', which alludes to the fin de siècle concerns with evolution (16). She claims that the old man's bones were 'audibly shattered', which is an example of sound imagery and hyperbole (16). This makes the enormity of the crime seem even greater, even if it makes her testimony a little less credible.

The dead man is identified as Sir Danvers Carew by Utterson, who is summoned to the police station. Utterson also recognises the murder weapon as a stick that he 'had himself presented many years before to Henry Jekyll' (17).

Meanwhile, the setting is a pea-souper, or a heavy poisonous fog that existed in London at that time. Through pathetic fallacy, the idea that this case is anything but clearcut is emphasised.

Utterson does know that Hyde resides in Soho, so visits this abode. The lawyer notes the 'dingy street' with 'penny numbers' or cheap literature amongst other things (17). This portrays Utterson as something of a snob, as we are seeing the scene from his perspective.

The narrator is quick to judge Hyde's landlady, describing her as having 'an evil face, smoothed by hypocrisy' (17). We can guess that Utterson is the focaliser in this chapter. Utterson introduces police 'Inspector Newcomen' to the woman, whose face flashes with 'odious joy' (17). That oxymoron sums up how deep down she does not want to speak to the police, yet on the surface she displays a polite manner.

9-1 GCSE REVISION NOTES – JEKYLL & HYDE

Chapter Five

At the start of the chapter entitled: 'Incident of the Letter', we follow Utterson, who is negotiating his way to Jekyll's 'building which was indifferently known as the laboratory or the dissecting rooms' (19). The reader may get the feeling that some diabolical experimenting is going on there, although the narrator adds that Jekyll is more focused on the 'chemical rather than anatomical' aspects of science (19). This rules out the possibility of a Frankenstein's monster being created with discarded bits of human anatomy.

However, Jekyll is looking 'deadly sick', a bit like Victor Frankenstein, who likewise became obsessed with his experiments and his creation (19). The reader may feel Jekyll is sick with worry, for he produces a letter written by Hyde which he has 'received' (20). He asks for advice as to what to do about it. Strangely, he claims that he has 'burned' the envelope; it is difficult to comprehend why he would do that if he is trying to help bring Hyde to justice (20). Jekyll feels he has 'had a lesson' and vows to have nothing more to do with Hyde, much to Utterson's relief (20).

However, Utterson still wonders about the letter, so once home he asks for Mr Guest's comments on it. Fortunately, Guest is a 'great student' of graphology, a pseudo-science that claims to gauge personality through the analysis of writing (21).

Guest concludes that 'there's a rather singular resemblance' to Jekyll's handwriting, although it's 'differently sloped' (22). This prompts Utterson to assume that Jekyll is forging 'for a murderer' (22). It adds to the tension and the mystery as the reader wants to know why Jekyll would do such a thing, or whether or not Utterson is mistaken.

9-1 GCSE REVISION NOTES – JEKYLL & HYDE

Chapter Six

In the chapter entitled 'Remarkable Incident of Dr Lanyon', we hear that Hyde has disappeared. Hyde's 'past' is 'unearthed', foreshadowing his possible death as the word 'earth' can be associated with burial (22).

Although Jekyll has become more sociable since Hyde's disappearance, by 12th January he has become something of a recluse again. The wintry time setting implies that Jekyll could be near death.

Meanwhile, Lanyon has 'his death-warrant written legibly upon his face' (23). The sick doctor, suffering from 'shock', says he want to 'hear no more of Dr Jekyll', although Utterson tells Lanyon that 'Jekyll is ill, too' (23).

Utterson writes to Jekyll asking for an explanation 'of this unhappy break with Lanyon' (24). Jekyll replies that if he is 'the chief of sinners', then he is 'the chief of sufferers also' (24). This comment deepens the mystery.

When Lanyon dies, the tension is dramatically increased by his letter to Utterson, which says: 'PRIVATE: for the hands of J.G. Utterson ALONE, and in the case of his predecease to be destroyed unread' (24). Inside that is another envelope that says: 'Not to be opened till the death or disappearance of Dr Henry Jekyll' (24). The contents are veiled in secrecy adding to the mystery.

Utterson manages to overcome his curiosity and consequently 'the packet slept in the inmost corner of his private safe' (25). The use of personification adds to the idea that the secret is alive and only lying dormant for now. Again, this adds to the tension.

9-1 GCSE REVISION NOTES – JEKYLL & HYDE

Chapter Seven

In this short chapter entitled: 'Incident at the Window', we feel sympathy for Jekyll from Utterson's perspective (25). Utterson admits: 'I am uneasy about poor Jekyll' (25). By simply adding the adjective 'poor', the reader is subtly manipulated into feeling that Jekyll is a victim.

Meanwhile, through the narrative technique of objective correlative, we learn about Jekyll's state of mind, which is mirrored by the scene that surrounds him. We learn that 'the sky' is 'still bright with sunset' (25). It seems as if Jekyll is sinking like the sun in the sky.

The simile 'like some disconsolate prisoner' aptly describes Jekyll (26). It implies that Jekyll is still under the influence of Hyde and the use of gothic terminology reinforces that idea. Jekyll tries to communicate 'with a smile', when addressed by his friends, but eventually ends the conversation with an expression of such abject terror and despair' (26). We, as readers, sympathise with Jekyll's plight.

Chapter Eight

This climactic chapter entitled: 'The Last Night' begins with Jekyll's servant, Poole, visiting Utterson (26). Although Utterson asks Poole to be 'explicit' about the situation regarding his master, the servant is unable to fully explain it (27). This ties in with the idea that much of the horror in the gothic genre is caused by unspeakable acts. Tension is added to the narrative, as the reader is left wondering exactly what has happened.

Utterson decides to accompany Poole back to Jekyll's house. On his arrival, it is noted that the servants are 'huddled together like a flock of sheep' (28). This portrays the lower classes as helpless followers, who are as innocent as frightened animals. All they need is leadership, which is not being offered by their master.

Even Jekyll's 'voice' has changed, according to Poole (29). From Poole's comment, Utterson concludes Jekyll has been murderered and that 'the murderer' is still there (29). Meanwhile, the reader can draw his or her own conclusions, which adds to the mystery.

As the narrative slowly unravels, it seems that the murderer must be Hyde. Poole says his master 'is a tall fine build of a man', whereas what he has seen instead is 'more of a dwarf' (30). Utterson decides it is his 'duty to make certain' of the truth (30). At this stage, he believes that 'poor Harry [Jekyll] is killed' and that 'his murderer [...] is still lurking in his victim's room' (31). The word 'lurking' makes the murderer's presence seem all the more ominous, as if he is looking to stalk another victim. However, the reader may feel the murderer is also a

9-1 GCSE REVISION NOTES – JEKYLL & HYDE

victim of sorts. He is clearly suffering, as Poole describes him as 'weeping like a woman' (32).

Using words associated with burial, the narrative describes how Poole 'disinterred the axe' in order to break down Jekyll's door (32). This language is typically gothic and adds to the idea that death awaits them inside the locked room.

Indeed, inside they see 'the body of a man sorely contorted and still twitching' (33). The narrative maintains tension by using a slow exposition, as it is only by turning the body on 'its back' that they discover that it is 'the face of Edward Hyde' (33).

It seems as if Hyde may have poisoned himself with cyanide, which would explain 'the strong smell of kernels that hung upon the air' (33). We learn that there is evidence of 'chemical work' with 'various measured heaps of some white salt being laid on glass saucers' (34). This provides the reader with another clue as to what has caused Hyde's demise.

More clues without answers follow, as Utterson picks up 'a will' in which he is named as Jekyll's beneficiary. Then he reads a letter instructing him to 'first read the narrative which Lanyon [...] placed in his hands' (35). Finally, Utterson picks up 'a third enclosure' or envelope, which he is taking back to his office to read (35). This leaves the chapter on a cliffhanger, as the reader wonders what Utterson will discover.

Chapter Nine

A new narrator takes over, in a chapter which is unsurprisingly entitled: 'Dr Lanyon's Narrative' (36). Now we find out about events from a first-person perspective, which may add realism and absorb the reader more. Generally, first-person narratives are considered more unreliable and biased, but Lanyon's profession should make his account reasonably objective.

After receiving Jekyll's letter, Lanyon's scientific opinion is the sender is 'insane' (37). However, he admits he does not completely understand 'this farrago', which in this case is a confused mixture of what he thinks might be fiction with fact (37).

Nevertheless, Lanyon follows Jekyll's instructions, emptying out the contents of 'the drawer' from 'the press marked E' (38). The reader can speculate as to what 'E' stands for. It could be 'Edward' possibly, or even 'evolution'.

After his return to his home in Cavendish Square, Lanyon is visited by Hyde at just after 'twelve o'clock' (38). This midnight visitation does not bode well, as the time setting suggests that evil is intruding on his home. This impression is added to by Hyde making 'greater haste' after spotting a policeman 'advancing with his bull's eye', or lantern, 'open' (38).

Hyde is full of 'impatience' and asks for 'a graduated glass' to mix the chemicals which Lanyon has brought back from Jekyll's laboratory (39). Before he drinks his concoction, Hyde asks Lanyon if 'the greed of curiosity' is in 'command' of him (40). By that, Hyde is asking whether it would be best to

9-1 GCSE REVISION NOTES – JEKYLL & HYDE

satisfy Lanyon's curiosity or leave him in blissful ignorance. This links to the idea of the Biblical 'Tree of Knowledge', meaning that some things are better left unknown. Christopher Marlowe wrote on a similar theme in the sixteenth century.

It transpires that Lanyon was wrong not to heed Hyde's warning, for he 'screamed' when he saw that Hyde had been transformed into Henry Jekyll, 'like a man restored from death', after taking the potion (41).

Chapter Ten

The final chapter is also written in the first-person, and it is entitled: 'Henry Jekyll's Full Statement of the Case' (41). In it, Jekyll reveals that one of his 'worst' faults is 'a certain impatient gaiety of disposition' (42). As Hyde is portrayed as impatient as well, it shows the reader that Jekyll's darker side was always living within him, even before he started taking potions to fully release his dark side.

He reveals that Hyde 'bore the stamp, of lower elements' in his 'soul' (43). On observing Hyde's appearance, Jekyll is aware that he 'had lost in stature' (44). This is an example of a pun, for stature refers to height as well as reputation; Jekyll has lost both by becoming in Hyde.

Jekyll likens his position to that of 'the captives of Philippi', who were released from prison by Roman leaders Anthony and Octavia in AD42, although there was a danger they might fight again for the opposition (45). This simile shows how dangerous it is for Jekyll to release Hyde, who feels he does not owe his loyalty in return.

The narrative changes to a third-person perspective, reflecting Jekyll's failure to take responsibility for his alter-ego's actions. He admits that 'his conscience slumbered' (46). The personification of his conscience emphasises how remiss his good side is, in allowing Hyde to take over consciousness.

Metaphorically, Jekyll has been going backwards through evolution to a more selfish, ape-like state. This is represented literally by his admission that 'by sloping' his 'own hand

9-1 GCSE REVISION NOTES – JEKYLL & HYDE

backwards', he could supply his 'double with a signature' (47). Furthermore, he horrifically describes Hyde's hand as 'lean, corded, knuckly, of a dusky pallor, and thickly shaded with a swart growth of hair' (47). This relates to Victorian evolutionary preoccupations that humans are the distant relatives of apes.

Jekyll admits the writing was on the wall, when he had 'gone to bed Henry Jekyll' and 'had awakened Edward Hyde' (47). He describes it as 'like the Babylonian finger' (48). This Biblical simile alludes to an incident at King Belshazzar's feast, when a hand appeared and began writing on the palace wall (signifying the end for the under-siege Babylon).

Although Jekyll desperately tries to regain control, he cannot bring himself to give up 'the house in Soho' or 'the clothes of Edward Hyde' (49). Fuelled by the guilt of what Hyde had done, Jekyll manages to labour 'to relieve suffering' (50). Inevitably, Jekyll feels like succumbing to temptation as he sits in Regent's Park, a significant location for it houses the animals of London Zoo. Similarly, the animal Hyde is caged inside Jekyll, who is like his zoo keeper.

The next thing Jekyll knows is the hand that lays on his knee is 'corded and hairy', signifying a transformation to Hyde (51).

There seems to be something natural and elemental about being Hyde, as the 'fear and hatred' that rage 'within him' are 'like a tempest' (52). While tempests are unwelcome, they are a natural phenomenon. However, they cause widespread devastation making it an apt simile to describe Hyde.

Hyde is described as 'closer than a wife' and laying 'caged in his flesh', struggling 'to be born' (53). Like a destructive child,

Hyde grows, while the creative father, Jekyll, diminishes. Jekyll disapproves of Hyde's 'apelike tricks', but is too weak and powerless to do anything about it (54).

A lack of an unspecified 'salt' means that the magic potion can no longer be produced, leading to the demise of both Jekyll and Hyde.

On that note, Jekyll lays down his pen and seals his 'confession' (54). Jekyll goes to his grave feeling guilty for his sins, which gives the reader the chance to feel some sympathy for him.

9-1 GCSE REVISION NOTES – JEKYLL & HYDE

Essay writing tips

Use a variety of connectives

Have a look of this list of connectives. Which of these would you choose to use?

'ADDING' DISCOURSE MARKERS

- AND
- ALSO
- AS WELL AS
- MOREOVER
- TOO
- FURTHERMORE
- ADDITIONALLY

I hope you chose 'additionally', 'furthermore' and 'moreover'. Don't be afraid to use the lesser discourse markers, as they are also useful. Just avoid using those ones over and over again. I've seen essays from Key Stage 4 students that use the same discourse marker for the opening sentence of each paragraph! Needless to say, those essays didn't get great marks!

Okay, here are some more connectives for you to look at. Select the best ones.

'SEQUENCING' DISCOURSE MARKERS

- NEXT
- FIRSTLY
- SECONDLY
- THIRDLY
- FINALLY
- MEANWHILE
- AFTER
- THEN
- SUBSEQUENTLY

This time, I hope you chose 'subsequently' and 'meanwhile'.

Here are some more connectives for you to 'grade'!

'ILLUSTRATING / EXEMPLIFYING' DISCOURSE MARKERS

- FOR EXAMPLE
- SUCH AS
- FOR INSTANCE
- IN THE CASE OF
- AS REVEALED BY
- ILLUSTRATED BY

9-1 GCSE REVISION NOTES – JEKYLL & HYDE

I'd probably go for 'illustrated by' or even 'as exemplified by' (which is not in the list!). Please feel free to add your own examples to the lists. Strong connectives impress examiners. Don't forget it! That's why I want you to look at some more.

'CAUSE & EFFECT' DISCOURSE MARKERS

- BECAUSE
- SO
- THEREFORE
- THUS
- CONSEQUENTLY
- HENCE

I'm going for 'consequently' this time. How about you? What about the next batch?

'COMPARING' DISCOURSE MARKERS

- SIMILARLY
- LIKEWISE
- AS WITH
- LIKE
- EQUALLY
- IN THE SAME WAY

I'd choose 'similarly' this time. Still some more to go.

'QUALIFYING' DISCOURSE MARKERS

- BUT
- HOWEVER
- WHILE
- ALTHOUGH
- UNLESS
- EXCEPT
- APART FROM
- AS LONG AS

It's 'however' for me!

'CONTRASTING' DISCOURSE MARKERS

- WHEREAS
- INSTEAD OF
- ALTERNATIVELY
- OTHERWISE
- UNLIKE
- ON THE OTHER HAND

9-1 GCSE REVISION NOTES – JEKYLL & HYDE

- CONVERSELY

I'll take 'conversely' or 'alternatively' this time.

'EMPHASISING' DISCOURSE MARKERS

- ABOVE ALL
- IN PARTICULAR
- ESPECIALLY
- SIGNIFICANTLY
- INDEED
- NOTABLY

You can breathe a sigh of relief now! It's over! No more connectives. However, now I want to put our new found skills to use in our essays.

Useful information/Glossary

Allegory: extended metaphor, like the grim reaper representing death, e.g. Scrooge symbolizing capitalism.

Alliteration: same consonant sound repeating, e.g. 'She sells sea shells'.

Allusion: reference to another text/person/place/event.

Ascending tricolon: sentence with three parts, each increasing in power, e.g. 'ringing, drumming, shouting'.

Aside: character speaking so some characters cannot hear what is being said. Sometimes, an aside is directly to the audience. It's a dramatic technique which reveals the character's inner thoughts and feelings.

Assonance: same vowel sounds repeating, e.g. 'Oh no, won't Joe go?'

Bathos: abrupt change from sublime to ridiculous for humorous effect.

Blank verse: lines of unrhymed iambic pentameter.

Compressed time: when the narrative is fast-forwarding through the action.

Descending tricolon: sentence with three parts, each decreasing in power, e.g. 'shouting, talking, whispering'.

Denouement: tying up loose ends, the resolution.

Diction: choice of words or vocabulary.

Didactic: used to describe literature designed to inform, instruct or pass on a moral message.

Dilated time: opposite compressed time, here the narrative is in slow motion.

9-1 GCSE REVISION NOTES – JEKYLL & HYDE

Direct address: second person narrative, predominantly using the personal pronoun 'you'.

Dramatic action verb: manifests itself in physical action, e.g. I punched him in the face.

Dramatic irony: audience knows something that the character is unaware of.

Ellipsis: leaving out part of the story and allowing the reader to fill in the narrative gap.

End-stopped lines: poetic lines that end with punctuation.

Epistolary: letter or correspondence-driven narrative.

Flashback/Analepsis: going back in time to the past, interrupting the chronological sequence.

Flashforward/Prolepsis: going forward in time to the future, interrupting the chronological sequence.

Foreshadowing/Adumbrating: suggestion of plot developments that will occur later in the narrative.

Gothic: another strand of Romanticism, typically with a wild setting, a sensitive heroine, an older man with a 'piercing gaze', discontinuous structure, doppelgangers, guilt and the 'unspeakable' (according to Eve Kosofsky Sedgwick).

Hamartia: character flaw, leading to that character's downfall.

Hyperbole: exaggeration for effect.

Iambic pentameter: a line of ten syllables beginning with a lighter stress alternating with a heavier stress in its perfect form, which sounds like a heartbeat. The stress falls on the even syllables, numbers: 2, 4, 6, 8 and 10, e.g. 'When now I think you can behold such sights'.

Intertextuality: links to other literary texts.

Irony: amusing or cruel reversal of expected outcome or words meaning the opposite to their literal meaning.

Metafiction/Romantic irony: self-conscious exposure of the devices used to create 'the truth' within a work of fiction.

Motif: recurring image use of language or idea that connects the narrative together and creates a theme or mood, e.g. 'green light' in *The Great Gatsby*.

Objective correlative: external features of the scene mirroring the feelings of a character.

Oxymoron: contradictory terms combined, e.g. deafening silence.

Pastiche: imitation of another's work.

Pathetic fallacy: a form of personification whereby inanimate objects show human attributes, e.g. 'the sea smiled benignly'. The originator of the term, John Ruskin in 1856, used 'the cruel, crawling foam', from Kingsley's *The Sands of Dee*, as an example to clarify what he meant by the 'morbid' nature of pathetic fallacy.

Personification: concrete or abstract object made human, often simply achieved by using a capital letter or a personal pronoun, e.g. 'Nature', or describing a ship as 'she'.

Pun/Double entendre: a word with a double meaning, usually employed in witty wordplay but not always.

Retrospective: account of events after they have occurred.

Romanticism: genre celebrating the power of imagination, spriritualism and nature.

Semantic/lexical field: related words about a single concept, e.g. king, queen and prince are all concerned with royalty.

9-1 GCSE REVISION NOTES – JEKYLL & HYDE

Soliloquy: character thinks aloud, but is not heard by other characters (unlike in a monologue) giving the audience access to inner thoughts and feelings.

Style: choice of language, form and structure, and effects produced.

Synecdoche: one part of something referring to the whole, e.g. Carker's teeth represent him in *Dombey and Son*.

Syntax: the way words and sentences are placed together.

Tetracolon climax: sentence with four parts, culminating with the last part, e.g. 'I have nothing to offer but blood, toil, tears, and sweat ' (Winston Churchill).

ABOUT THE AUTHOR

Joe Broadfoot is a secondary school teacher of English and a soccer journalist, who also writes fiction and literary criticism. His former experiences as a DJ took him to far-flung places such as Tokyo, Kobe, Beijing, Hong Kong, Jakarta, Cairo, Dubai, Cannes, Oslo, Bergen and Bodo. He is now PGCE and CELTA-qualified with QTS, a first-class honours degree in Literature and an MA in Victorian Studies (majoring in Charles Dickens). Drama is close to his heart as he acted in 'Macbeth' and 'A Midsummer Night's Dream' at the Royal Northern College of Music in Manchester. More recently, he has been teaching 'A' Level and GCSE English Literature and IGCSE and GCSE English Language to students at secondary schools in Buckinghamshire, Kent and in south and west London.

Printed in Great Britain
by Amazon